later the Normans built a massive castle keep at Colchester, the largest in Europe, and a thriving medieval town grew up based on the cloth trade. The town survived the devastation of the Black Death and a major siege during the English Civil War. By the Victorian period its growth had taken a different turn, and the town

became known for garrison and engine In recent years Col changed again, with ments such as the U Much of Colchester's continuing attraction as a place to work, live in or visit lies in its well-preserved historic character. We hope this guide will help you to enjoy that heritage today.

today.

Why Colchester is Britain's oldest recorded town

The earliest record of Colchester's existence is a reference by the Roman writer Pliny the Elder in AD77. In describing the location of the island of Anglesey, he wrote that 'it is about 200 miles from Camulodunum, a town in Britain'. This is the first known reference to any named settlement in this country. Pliny, shown here in a medieval manuscript illustration, died in AD79, one of the victims of the eruption of Mount Vesuvius which destroyed Pompeii.

The Colchester Borough Arms

The borough arms first appears on the charter granted to the borough in 1413 by King Henry V. The green cross represents the True Cross and is depicted as having green, living shoots. The True Cross, as legend has it, was found by St Helena, who was born in Colchester and was the mother of Constantine. The cross bears three iron nails and bears the crowns of the three kings whose relics she also found. The red background represents the blood of Christ.

FRONT COVER Roman bronze statue of Mercury (left), half-timbered cottages by the Colne (top), the Jumbo water tower (centre left), a gold coin of Cunobelin (centre right) and Colchester Castle (below).
THIS PAGE Colchester Castle and Castle Park.

Camulodunum

Cunobelin, Shakespeare's Cymbeline, ruled from about AD5 to AD40. His wealth and status are well illustrated by the gold coins he issued, which carry the CVNO of his name (*above*) and the CAMV of Camulodunum (*cover*).

Colchester is famous as a Roman town, but its origins pre-date the Romans. Two thousand years ago much of the area now covered by Essex and Suffolk was occupied by the Trinovantes tribe. Towards the end of the first century BC the Trinovantes built up a settlement on the River Colne, which became known as Camulodunum, meaning 'Fortress of Camulos', a Celtic war god. Camulodunum was not a town in the modern sense, but was more like a large country estate. It covered a huge area of some 12 square miles (31 km²) and included commercial, industrial and farming settlements as well as the royal household. All of

them were enclosed and protected by an elaborate system of earthworks (dykes), much of which survives today. The Romans were well aware of the growing importance of Camulodunum and referred to its powerful ruler Cunobelin as King of the Britons. Cunobelin's death, around AD40, rekindled thoughts of invasion, previously planned by Augustus and Gaius (Caligula). When the Roman army did arrive in AD43, the capture of Camulodunum was its principal objective.

BELOW A group of Trinovantes running and riding through the defensive earthworks of Camulodunum to repel an attack.

Roman Colchester

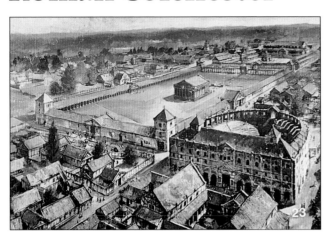

LEFT **Roman Colchester in about AD 150, looking south-east. The theatre is on the right with the temple precinct beyond.**

The Roman Emperor Claudius spent just sixteen days in Britain, long enough to lead his troops into Camulodunum and receive the submission of several British kings. The Roman army then built a legionary fortress on the highest ground inside Camulodunum, the site of the present town centre. The High Street still follows the central axis of the original fortress while the intersection of Head Street and North Hill marks a main crossroads of the subsequent Roman town.

As the Roman army moved north to conquer the rest of Britain, new military bases were built on the way. By AD49 the fortress at Camulodunum had been turned into a civilian

The Roman Emperor Claudius saw the conquest of Britain as an opportunity to boost his own reputation at home by extending the Empire. He was not present when his armies landed in Kent, but arrived in time to make a triumphal entrance into Camulodunum accompanied by elephants, animals the Britons would never have seen before.

LEFT **The gravestone of Marcus Favonius Facilis, which can be seen in the Castle Museum. He was a Roman centurion who died at Colchester. The illustration on the far left is a reconstruction of how he would have looked in life.**

3

Our knowledge of Boudica comes mainly from the Roman writer Tacitus. Until recently she was better known as Boadicea, but this is now thought to be a medieval scribe's error which was perpetuated. Her name translates as Victoria. No contemporary pictures of her exist, and she has become a mythical figure. This romantic Victorian image of her is on a stained glass window in Colchester Town Hall.

settlement named Colonia Claudia after the Emperor, and this became the first capital of the new Roman province of Britannia.

The colonia was populated mainly by retired soldiers, whose role was to spread Roman civilisation and keep an eye on the natives. Many of the military buildings were retained and converted, but the legionary defences were dismantled, leaving the town fatally unprotected. Large public buildings were erected, including a theatre and a senate house. Grandest of all was the **Temple of Claudius**, built to worship the Emperor after his death in AD54, when he was made a god. The foundations of the temple still survive underneath Colchester Castle and can be visited on guided tours.

Roman Colchester was virtually destroyed only a few years after the town was founded. In AD60 Queen Boudica of the Iceni, the native tribe living in the Norfolk area, led a major rebellion against Roman rule. Prasutagus, the Iceni king, had been one of the British rulers who submitted to Claudius in AD43. After his death the Romans assaulted his widow Boudica and her daughters, refusing to accept the

BELOW **The Roman town, including the Temple of Claudius, is destroyed by Boudica's followers in AD60.**

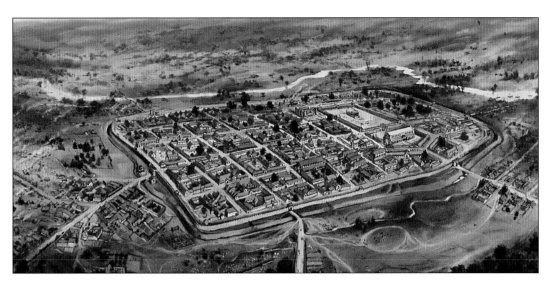

women as the king's heirs.

A revolt erupted and Boudica led her followers against the Roman capital at Camulodunum. Here the Iceni joined forces with the Trinovantes to attack and burn the undefended town. Those colonists who survived the initial assault retreated into the town's largest building, the Temple of Claudius, but they could only hold out for a couple of days. The Temple, which had been paid for through heavy local taxes and built with the slave labour of the Britons, was a particular focus of hatred. It too was burnt and all the defenders slaughtered.

Boudica was not defeated until her rather disorganised followers faced a disciplined Roman army in battle. By then they had destroyed two more Roman towns, at London and St Albans. Despite the scale of the destruction, Colchester was quickly rebuilt but this time enclosed by a substantial defensive wall. Some two-thirds of this still stand, the oldest town wall in Britain. Particularly noteworthy is the **Balkerne Gate**, the original main entrance to the town, which probably began as a triumphal arch celebrating the conquest by Claudius.

Roman Colchester lasted at least 400 years. Inevitably the distinction between conquerors and conquered faded. To be Roman was to be civilised, particularly with the conferring of Roman citizenship on all free-born people in the Empire.

This is well illustrated by the **Gosbecks site** on the south-western edge of the modern town. Gosbecks was Cunobelin's royal seat at Camulodunum. After the Roman invasion, Gosbecks was allowed to continue as a flourishing native centre, watched over initially by a Roman fort which could house 500 soldiers. Nearby the largest of the five known Roman theatres in Britain was built, with seating for up to 5,000 people. There was also an impressive Romano-Celtic temple complex. The discovery nearby of the Colchester Mercury, the finest bronze figure from Roman Britain, shows that even native religion was becoming Romanised. Gosbecks is now being preserved as an **Archaeological Park**, and its various historic features are explained on site.

Inevitably the walled colonia became the real centre of population. At its peak the territorium would have had a population of at least

ABOVE Roman Colchester in about AD250, rebuilt after the Boudican rebellion with a defensive wall around the town.

ABOVE Detail from the Middleborough Mosaic, the largest decorated floor found in Colchester, which can be seen in Colchester Castle Museum.

RIGHT **Only a low mound survives on the site of the huge Roman theatre at Gosbecks, but the building's position and plan are now accurately marked out in the new Archaeological Park.**

BELOW **Mercury, the finest Roman bronze figure discovered in Britain, was found on the Gosbecks site and can now be seen in the Castle Museum.**

RIGHT **A finely decorated Roman pot, known as the Colchester Vase, showing gladiatorial combat.**

15,000, based on 2000 settlers in the Colonia.

Archaeological excavations over the last seventy years have revealed a town of importance and sophistication. It was a consumer society catered for by mass-production and international trade. There was a theatre, at least eight temples, a public water supply, over forty pottery kilns, glass and metal manufacturers and a major industrial complex, doubtless using slave labour. Large town-houses have been uncovered with underfloor heating and many fine decorated mosaic floors – clear indications of wealth and luxury living.

Extensive cemeteries in the south and west of the town have produced elaborate grave goods of amazing variety and quality. These can now be seen amongst the internationally important archaeological collections of the **Castle Museum**. On the edge of the main cemetery, at Butt Road, the earliest known **Christian church** in Britain, dating from the fourth century, has been uncovered. Its foundations are now displayed beside the police station on Southway.

From the fourth century onwards Roman Britain became increasingly subject to Saxon raids across the North Sea. We do not know whether there was a sudden, violent end to the Romano-British administration but it is clear that by AD410 Britain had effectively ceased to be part of the Roman Empire.

By the fifth century many of the Saxon raiders were settling permanently in this country. The remains of three Saxon huts have been discovered within Colchester's walls, but if town life did continue in the Dark Ages it would have been very different to the Roman period. Much of the town may have been un-occupied, and the Roman buildings were left to decay.

Medieval Colchester

LEFT **The massive walls of the castle keep are more than 3 m thick (around 10 ft).**

Eudo de Rie, Steward (or Dapifer) to William the Conqueror and head of the royal household through three reigns. As the first Constable of the Castle, he was, in effect, governor of the town. Eudo established the Abbey of St John and a leper hospital just outside the town. This fanciful Victorian statue of him is on the Town Hall.

of the ruined Roman town can be seen put to new use.

The victory of William the Conqueror at the Battle of Hastings in 1066 brought Anglo-Saxon England to an abrupt end. The Normans found a busy port and market town at Colchester, and chose it as the site for one of the first stone castles in England. Construction of **Colchester Castle** began within ten years of the conquest, pre-dating both the Tower of London and Norwich Castle.

The massive foundations of the ruined Roman Temple of Claudius formed a convenient base for the castle keep, which is consequently the largest ever built by the Normans. Its purpose was both to control the town and surrounding area and to act as a defence against seaborne invasion from Scandinavia. In practice it saw military action only once, in 1216, when King John besieged the castle and recaptured it from French mercenary troops sent to aid his rebellious barons.

The long entry for Colchester in the 'Domesday Book' (1086) catalogues a small but wealthy town. A new port was established at the Hythe before 1200, thriving on international trade, and in 1189 the town received its first

There are no written records to shed light on life in Colchester in the 500 years after the end of Roman rule. The next documented event was in 917 when the Wessex King Edward the Elder, son of Alfred the Great, expelled a Danish garrison that was occupying the town. Edward repaired Colchester's walls and effectively re-established the town.

The Saxons may have given Colchester its modern name, which derives from Colneceaster, meaning 'Fortress on the Colne'. Only one of their buildings, the tower of **Holy Trinity Church**, still stands. This dates from about 1000 and is the earliest surviving medieval building in Colchester in which the brick and tile

Royal Charter, from King Richard I. This gave the wealthier citizens various rights to manage local affairs, including markets, the Colne fisheries and judicial arrangements. These privileges were confirmed and extended by successive charters throughout the Medieval period.

Medieval Colchester had a number of religious foundations, including **St Botolph's Priory**, the first Augustinian house in England, and **St John's Abbey**. Today the impressive ruins of the great church at St Botolph's only hint at the scale of the medieval priory, while of St John's Abbey some long sections of the precinct wall and the later Tudor gatehouse survive.

In 1348 at least a quarter of Colchester's population died of the plague as the

LEFT The ruins of St Botolph's Priory Church today and *(ABOVE)* a reconstruction showing the church as it would have appeared in about 1200.

Black Death decimated Western Europe. The town not only survived this crisis but soon experienced a new golden age as trade recovered and the local cloth industry boomed.

RIGHT The Royal Charter granted to Colchester by King Henry V in 1413. It shows the town's patron saint Helena, with her son Constantine the Great. Below her is the earliest-known representation of the borough's coat of arms.

BELOW The medieval town seal of Colchester, used on official civic documents.

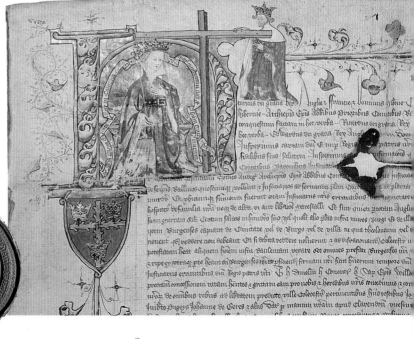

Tudor Colchester

ABOVE **Tymperleys, which dates back to about 1500, is one of many early timber-framed buildings which survive today in Colchester.**

William Gilberd, born in Colchester in 1544, became Chief Physician to Queen Elizabeth I, but is best known as a pioneer investigator of electricity. He coined the word 'electric' and conducted some of the first real experiments in electromagnetism. Tymperleys, in Trinity Street, was part of his family property in Colchester. Gilberd died in 1603 and is buried in the chancel of Holy Trinity Church.

National political and religious struggles were reflected in dramatic local events in the sixteenth century. St Botolph's Priory and St John's Abbey were both closed down in King Henry VIII's dissolution of the monasteries in the 1550s. In the reign of his zealous Catholic daughter Queen Mary, forty Protestants from Colchester and the surrounding district were burnt alive at the stake as heretics, a larger proportion, relative to population, than in any other town in England.

When Mary was succeeded as Queen by her Protestant sister Elizabeth, Colchester became a haven for Protestants fleeing from Flanders, where they had been defeated in a rebellion against Catholic Spain. Colchester Corporation petitioned the Queen to allow a large number of Dutch refugees to settle in the town, and more than 500 had arrived by 1575. Many of them were skilled weavers, and it was through this Dutch community that Colchester became famous for high-quality cloths known as bays and says. The district where most of the Flemish weavers lived and worked is known to this day as the **Dutch Quarter**, and many of their timber-framed houses still stand in this historic part of the town.

LEFT **A lead seal used to identify shipments of Colchester bays and says.**

ABOVE **Six Protestants accused of heresy are burnt at the stake in Colchester in 1556.**

Stuart Colchester

Matthew Hopkins from Mistley, near Colchester, achieved notoriety in the 1640s during the social upheavals of the English Civil War. He became known as the Witchfinder General, extracting confessions from women accused of witchcraft. **Some of these interrogations took place in the prisons of Colchester Castle.**

England was divided by a bitter Civil War in the mid-seventeenth century that arose out of the power struggle between King and Parliament. Colchester became a focus of the final phase of the conflict in 1648 when the town was seized by a Royalist force and besieged for eleven weeks by a Parliamentary army. The citizens of Colchester were pawns in a lethal battle: outside they were fired on, inside they starved. There is no accurate tally of the victims but it is certain that hundreds of townspeople died along with the soldiers of both sides.

After the inevitable surrender, two of the Royalist commanders, Lucas and Lisle, were executed by firing squad outside the castle. Colchester was left with its buildings in ruins, its cloth trade disrupted and its

THE LOYALL SACRIFICE.

ABOVE **The execution of Sir Charles Lucas and Sir George Lisle, two of the Royalist commanders shot after the Siege of Colchester in 1648.**

ABOVE **Bullet holes from the 1648 siege can still be seen in the Siege House on East Street.**

walls breached. The physical damage can still be seen in many places, including the ruins of **St Botolph's Priory Church** and the tower of **St Mary at the Walls Church**, both destroyed by cannon fire, the bullet holes in the **Siege House** and the large sections of the **town wall** later repaired in brick.

Less than twenty years after the Siege, Colchester was hit by the Great Plague. More than 4,000 Colcestrians, over half the town's population, died in the worst epidemic in modern England, but once again Colchester made a remarkable recovery from disaster.

Georgian Colchester

ABOVE **A panorama of Colchester from the north in 1724.**

Colchester was still a prosperous town in the early 1700s. Visitors commented favourably on its broad High Street, paved sidewalks and new brick houses. **Hollytrees** and **The Minories**, now a museum and art gallery respectively, are two of the surviving Georgian mansions that confirm the wealth and taste of the town's leading citizens in this period. By contrast, John Wesley, founder of the Methodist Church, who made several preaching visits to Colchester, encountered great poverty as well. The prison reformer John Howard was critical of the grim conditions he found in the castle, then still in use as a gaol.

The famous local bay and say cloth industry went into terminal decline in the eighteenth century. However, Colchester's roller-coaster fortunes took another upward turn in the late 1700s when an agricultural boom in Essex brought new prosperity to the town's markets and trade. The end of the traditional cloth industry in Colchester and the rise of new agricultural trade was marked both physically and symbolically by the opening of a grand new **Corn Exchange** in 1820. It was on the site, at the western end of the High Street, formerly occupied by the Dutch Bay Hall.

BELOW **Hollytrees, the town's finest Georgian mansion, built in 1718.**

Sisters Jane and Ann Taylor came to live in Colchester with their family as teenagers in 1796. Both soon began writing and had a number of poems and hymns for children published. None of their compositions is familiar to us today except one poem whose opening lines are known throughout the English-speaking world: 'Twinkle, twinkle little star, how I wonder what you are ...'

LEFT **Colchester High Street in the 1820s, with the new Corn Exchange on the left.**

Victorian Colchester

ABOVE **The heavy machine shop at Paxman's engineering works in 1903.**

ABOVE **Colchester Town Hall, completed in 1902.**

During the Napoleonic wars large numbers of soldiers were garrisoned at Colchester because of the new invasion threat. They left again after the peace in 1815, but forty years later a permanent garrison was established, initially in wooden huts, and the army has remained an important feature of Colchester's life ever since. A tangible link with those mid-Victorian origins is the simple but functional white wooden **Garrison Church** in Military Road, put up in 1856 and in regular use for worship ever since.

The railway arrived in 1843, giving Colchester a rapid link with London and the rest of the country, though it had little immediate impact on the Victorian town. Colchester generated its own economic recovery in the late nineteenth century through a range of successful local enterprises: mills, clothing and boot factories, breweries and building firms. The most prominent of these new industries was engineering: Britannia machine tools, Mumford's marine engineers and Paxman's steam engines and boilers. Export-led, Paxman's was to be for almost a hundred years the town's largest employer.

LEFT **The great Victorian water tower built in 1882–3. It was soon known as Jumbo after the famous elephant at London Zoo, which had then just been sold, amid national protests, to the American circus showman P.T. Barnum.**

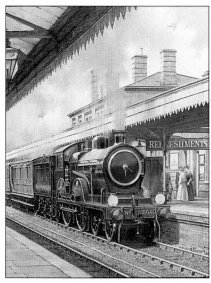

LEFT A Great Eastern Railway London express at Colchester North Station, 1910.

Victorian achievements. The first is the great water tower put up in 1882, which was soon known locally as **Jumbo** after the famous elephant at London Zoo. The second is the **Town Hall**, completed in 1902 and still the town's grandest building. Its elaborate ornamentation in stained glass and carved stone includes most of the key figures in Colchester's long history. It is a confident, if rose-tinted, celebration of the town's heritage, serving as a constant reminder of Colchester's historic past.

Charles Haddon Spurgeon (1834–92), born in Kelvedon, brought up on Hythe Hill, Colchester, became the greatest evangelical preacher of Victorian England. After being converted at the age of 15, he became a Baptist and a key figure in forging the links between Nonconformism and the Victorian Liberal Party. He founded the Metropolitan Tabernacle and Spurgeon's College, and he visited Colchester regularly. The small chapel in Artillery Street, the site of his conversion, is now the Spurgeon Memorial Chapel.

The company has continued to supply major contracts in recent years, including the diesel engines for British Rail's high-speed train fleet.

Colchester Borough Council, with the active assistance of these booming local industries, developed an impressive range of new public facilities in the late Victorian and Edwardian town. **Castle Park**, a public library, new schools and an electricity supply which also fed a council-run tramway system were all opened in this period. During the Victorian era the town's population had more than trebled, totalling 40,000 by 1901.

Two surviving landmarks on the Colchester skyline symbolise these

ABOVE A military parade on the Abbey Fields, c. 1900.

BELOW The Oyster Feast in the Moot Hall, 1904. This annual civic occasion still takes place every October.

LEFT On 22 April 1884 an earthquake struck the Colchester area. No-one was killed but there was widespread damage to buildings, including Peldon's Rose Inn, which was close to the epicentre. The *Peldon Rose* can still be visited today.

A Walk in Colchester

This walk, marked here as a yellow line   , around the historic town centre takes about
1½ hours, but can be shortened. A more detailed Town Trail leaflet is available from the Visitor
Information Centre. Guided walking tours led by Blue Badge Guides can also be booked at the
Visitor Information Centre.

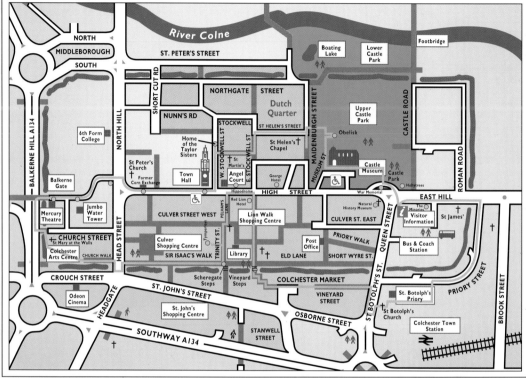

From the **Visitor Information Centre**, cross over
the road, past the **War Memorial**, unveiled in
1923, and into **Castle Park**, opened in 1892. Turn
left along the south front of **Colchester Castle**
(*below*), built from *c*. 1076 to 1125. Originally at
least one storey higher, it has been substantially
altered over the years. This now houses the award-
winning **Castle Museum**.

Turn right by the footbridge to the castle
entrance and walk around to the far (north) side of
the castle. An obelisk marks the spot where two of
the Royalist commanders were executed after the
Siege of Colchester (1648).

The grassy
bank here is part
of the original
castle defences.
Beyond it Castle
Park runs down
to and beyond
the River Colne.

Leave the park
by the nearest
exit, walk through the
alley and left into
Maidenburgh Street.
This is the **Dutch
Quarter** once lived in
by Flemish weavers.

The thirteenth-
century **St Helen's
Chapel** stands on the
corner. A little further
up the hill, part of the
remains of a **Roman Theatre** has been left

uncovered under number 74 Maidenburgh Street.
The outline of the theatre has been marked out in
darker paving in the road. Turn round and walk
back down the hill a little to turn left along
St Helen's Lane, left at the end and right through
the lane next to **St Martin's** churchyard. The
church is medieval, mostly fourteenth century.

Turn right down West Stockwell Street (*above*).
At numbers 11–12 you will find the home of the
Taylor sisters, composers of 'Twinkle Twinkle Little
Star'. Walk back up to the High Street, past a fine

fifteenth-century timber-framed house on the left. Notice the carved figures around the door.

The **Town Hall** *(left)*, completed in 1902, has a 50 m (about 164 ft) tower topped by a statue representing St Helena, patron saint of Colchester. Look up to see the statues of notable figures from Colchester's history, including Boudica (Boadicea).

Turn right along the High Street, passing under the colonnade of the former Essex and Suffolk Fire Office, built in 1820 as the **Corn Exchange**.

Cross over the top of North Hill. Most of the buildings lining the hill are eighteenth century or earlier, including **St Peter's Church** opposite, with its tower built in 1758. The large church clock is Victorian.

Walk down Balkerne Passage past the impressive water tower of 1882–3, known ever since as **Jumbo**. The **Mercury Theatre** nearby was opened in 1972. Beyond are the remains of the **Balkerne Gate** *(below)*, the largest surviving Roman gateway in Britain.

Go through the gate and turn left along Balkerne Hill, beside the **Roman wall**, denoted as an uneven brown line on the map. This is a particularly well-preserved stretch of the oldest town wall in the country.

Turn left up the steps to **St Mary at the Walls Church**, now the **Colchester Arts Centre**, and right through the churchyard and along Church Walk to Head Street. Cross over at the lights, turn left and first right and walk down Sir Isaac's Walk, passing the **Culver Shopping Centre** on your left.

Pause at **Scheregate Steps** *(top right)*, one of the medieval gateways cut through the Roman town wall to provide access to St John's Abbey. Turn left up Trinity Street. Approximately halfway up on the left is an archway, and through the archway is **Tymperleys**, a restored late fifteenth-century house which now contains a clock museum. Further up on the right is **Holy Trinity Church** *(centre right)*, with its Saxon tower.

Continue up Trinity Street and through Pelham's Lane, turning right into the High Street. The **Hippodrome** opposite, now a night club, was built as a theatre

in 1905. Further down on the same side is the **George Hotel**, an inn since the sixteenth century.

Walk down the High Street to the timber-framed **Red Lion Hotel**, also an inn since about 1500. Turn right into the arcade through to the modern **Lion Walk Shopping Centre**.

From the top of Vineyard Steps you can see the Tudor gatehouse of **St John's Abbey**. Go down the steps, or lift, to the car park, now the home of **Colchester Market** on Fridays and Saturdays. Notice another section of the Roman wall on the left.

Walk down Vineyard Street and right into St Botolph's Street. Cross at the lights, turn left then right into St Botolph's Church Walk, and left in front of the Norman-style **St Botolph's Church** (1837). The impressive ruins of **St Botolph's Priory Church** *(below)* lie alongside the present church, showing yet more recycling of Roman brick and tile.

Leave the churchyard by the far exit and turn right into Priory Street, passing sections of the town wall repaired in brick after the 1648 siege.

Turn left up East Hill past **St James's**, the town's largest medieval church. **The Minories**, on the left, now an art gallery, was rebuilt in 1776. Further up on the right is **Hollytrees**, built in 1718 and now a museum. Over the road is **All Saints' Church**, partly fifteenth century but mostly Victorian. It is now the **Natural History Museum** with a wildlife garden in the churchyard.

You are now back at the **Visitor Information Centre**.

A Cultural Centre

What was once the Roman capital of Britain is now acknowledged to be the 'Cultural Capital' of the County of Essex. Colchester has long been associated with fine arts and craftsmanship. Today the town is a thriving regional centre for the arts.

Taking a simple walk around the town centre, the visitor begins to get a flavour of the town's rich cultural identity as an architectural panorama is encountered in which beautiful buildings representing many periods cluster together.

Colchester is endowed with over a dozen museums and galleries. Dolls, toys and costume from yesteryear can be found in the delightful Georgian setting of **Hollytrees Museum**. A comprehensive collection of Colchester-made clocks, featured on the BBC's *Antiques Roadshow*, is elegantly housed in the fifteenth-century timber-framed **Tymperleys Clock Museum**. This

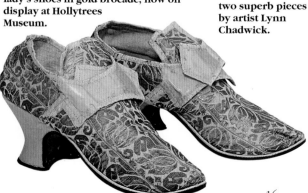

BELOW **Exquisite eighteenth-century lady's shoes in gold brocade, now on display at Hollytrees Museum.**

LEFT **This eight-day walnut longcase clock was made by Woodcock & Son around 1818. The decorative enamelled face commemorates the first balloon ascent from Colchester on 3 January 1783.**

collection of Colchester-made clocks, which date back to the late 1600s, was bequeathed to the town by Colchester businessman and horologist Bernard Mason and includes longcase clocks, watches and turret clocks as well as wall and spring clocks. Most notable are the precision regulators made by Joseph Banister with their mercury-filled glass pendulums.

Painting and artists have long been associated with this part of East Anglia. The lives and works of John Constable, Thomas Gainsborough and equestrian painter Sir Alfred

LEFT **Red Man** This specially commissioned work by artist Marc Fritzsche from our twin town of Wetzlar in Germany welcomes visitors to High Woods Country Park.

RIGHT **The garden at The Minories gallery provides an ideal setting for sculptures. Pictured here are two superb pieces by artist Lynn Chadwick.**

LEFT The Sensory Garden is a work of art in itself. Specially commissioned mosaics by ceramicist Marion Brandis, as well as seating and balustrading complete this delightful area of Castle Park.

John Constable This quintessentially English landscape-painter was born at East Bergholt on 11 June 1776 and exhibited his first work at the Royal Academy in 1802. He said of the Suffolk/Essex countryside: 'Those scenes made me a painter and I am grateful.' His most famous work, *The Hay Wain*, was painted in 1821 and can now be seen in the National Gallery. He was elected to full membership of the Royal Academy in 1829 and died in March 1837.

Munnings are strongly associated with local landscapes and traditions.

Twentieth-century painters such as John Nash, Lucien Pissarro and Cedric Morris also have Colchester connections. Nash and Morris were affiliated to the Colchester Arts Society, established in 1946, as was the pioneering design partnership of Henry Collins and Joyce Pallot.

Today there are many opportunities to purchase original paintings and prints by living artists as well as to watch craftspeople at work. **The Minories Art Gallery** has been home for over thirty-five years to a wide variety of twentieth-century exhibitions. The setting, an eighteenth-century town-house, includes a café and a delightful walled garden used for sculpture and outdoor exhibits in the summer months. The **Pam Schomberg Gallery**, featured in *Country Living*

BELOW A beautiful salt-glazed porcelain pelican jug by Anthony Theakston.

BELOW *My Wife, My Horse and Myself* by Sir Alfred Munnings, KCVO, PRA (1878–1959). Painted 1932–3, this oil on canvas was exhibited at the Royal Academy in 1939.

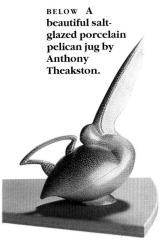

LEFT **Cuckoo Farm Studios is the location for some of the area's most exciting artists. Cuckoo Farm residents, Peter Jones' slip-cast stoneware vessels** (*LEFT*) **and** (*CENTRE*) **Sara Barker's hand-pierced aluminium jewellery with dyed nylon are sold all over the world.**

magazine, is the only Crafts Council-approved gallery in Essex – a cornucopia of contemporary British crafts, including stunningly crafted jewellery, hand-woven textiles and appliqué, colourful blown glass, exquisitely designed ceramics and delicately turned wood.

Colchester can be described as a gallery without walls as over the years the townscape and surrounding areas have been adorned by the works of art in many public and open spaces. The work of five contemporary British artists can be enjoyed in the **Sensory Garden** in Castle Park. Bold and colourful porcelain seats are set into raised circular beds containing more than 200 aromatic plants and shrubs.

Made in Colchester

Today many fine artists and crafts-people produce work from studios in and around Colchester. Many, trained

BELOW **The Mercury Theatre, a repertory theatre performing everything from comedy to Shakespearian tragedy.**

LEFT **Henry Collins' work often encapsulated Essex land- and seascapes and displays his interest in texture, collage and colour.**

ABOVE **Part of Colchester's Mayoral robes created by the Colchester Institute School of Art and Design for female mayors. The robes detail the town's connection with oysters through exquisite gold embroidery around the yoke.**

locally, have formed collectives. Artists' studios are run as small business units at **Cuckoo Farm** in Boxted Road, which also holds courses, workshops and exhibitions.

Colchester's arts products are more than just those to hang on a wall. **The Mercury Theatre** continues the tradition of fine live productions and performances established in 1937 by

ABOVE *A Colchester Symphony*, **specially commissioned from international film-music composer John Scott, is a musical portrait of Colchester's history in five movements.**

The Colchester Rep.

Signals Media Centre, an educational film and video company based in Colchester, has received international acclaim and won awards at the Berlin and San Francisco film festivals.

The arts scene in Colchester today is a lively one. This can be seen at a glance by flipping through the town's own 'Yellow Pages' for the arts, *The Colchester Arts Handbook*, which contains more than 500 entries, or by picking up a copy of the town's *Time Out* listing. Colchester boasts live entertainment virtually every night of the week at venues such as **Charter Hall, Mercury Theatre, Lakeside Theatre** and **Colchester Arts Centre**. Particularly noted for its network of live music venues, Colchester has attracted many international names in classical, jazz, folk and pop. The town has also proved to be a success-ful training ground for performers and new bands such as the award-winning Brit-pop band Blur.

19

Gardens and Events

ABOVE **The Ermine Street Guard re-enactors display the discipline and ingenuity of the Roman army.**

Surely the jewel in Colchester's crown is **Castle Park**. This distinguished Victorian park of 33 gently sloping acres (13.5 ha) now provides a natural venue for a wide range of events, fairs and festivals throughout the year. Listed as 'Grade Two' in the Register of Parks and Gardens as being of Special Historical Importance and much of it a Scheduled Ancient Monument, the park features a classic Victorian bandstand where a variety of live music can be heard on summer Sunday afternoons.

Castle Park hosts a wide variety of events every year. Colchester's heritage is celebrated through history 'fayres' and performances by historical re-enactment groups. Children's events also provide a lively atmosphere in the park. A natural theatre, the park offers an ideal venue for open-air concerts, which are highly popular with residents and visitors alike during the summer. The season is rounded off each year in November

LEFT **The Avignon Garden – just one of a number of formal gardens in Castle Park.**

BELOW **The Sensory Garden in Castle Park: a specially designed combination of textures, colours and perfumes.**

with the annual Bonfire Night fireworks display, featuring a procession of Guy Fawkes around the park.

Rich combinations of colour and texture can be found in a variety of formal gardens situated throughout the park. The spectacular Avignon Garden, named in honour of our twin town in France, can be found at the foot of the castle ramparts, a surviving earthwork that originally protected the keep. The Avignon Garden features an ever-changing display of colour throughout the year and is the perfect place to sit and watch the world go by. Our twin town in Germany, Wetzlar, has also been honoured with a delightful garden situated next to the Hollytrees Museum.

A recent addition to Castle Park is a garden to delight all the senses. Incorporating specially commissioned works of art, the Sensory Garden provides a unique blend of colours, textures, sights and perfumes. A stroll to Lower Castle Park takes you down

a winding path and through the Roman wall, past the bowling-greens and traditional boating-lake with its magnificent weeping willow tree and on to Colchester's county-standard cricket ground, situated alongside the River Colne. Essex County Cricket Club has been playing professional cricket in Castle Park most years since 1914. This area of the park is an ideal place to take river-side walks.

ABOVE **Castle Park Lodge, with the boating-lake in the background.**

CENTRE **The bandstand in Castle Park, still the venue for live music on summer Sunday afternoons.**

BELOW **The sound of leather on willow greets August visitors to Castle Park's county-standard cricket ground.**

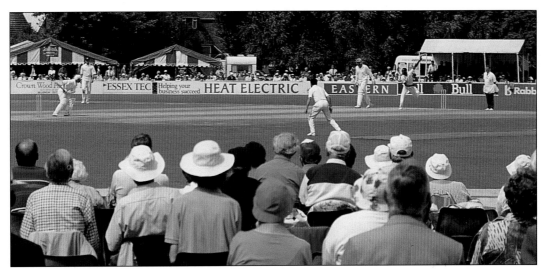

Colchester Today

The historic town of Colchester is today at the heart of a flourishing, modern borough, home to around 150,000 people. It is *the* major shopping and leisure centre for surrounding local communities and neighbouring smaller towns and villages.

Colchester is among the top few towns described as 'the most desirable places to live in Britain'. One of the reasons for this is the many unique and award-winning local leisure attractions. **Colchester Zoo**, a favourite of world-famous botanist David Bellamy, has one of England's finest zoological collections and is home to over 170 species. An internationally respected conservation centre, Colchester Zoo has often been voted Best Visitor Attraction in Essex.

Europe's finest rollerskating rink can be found at **Rollerworld**. Chosen for many years as the venue for the National Rollerskating Championships, Rollerworld's exquisite maple floor has been described by the World Champion skater Lee Taylor as the best in Britain. Also unique to Colchester is **Aqua Springs** at the town's major sporting venue, **Leisure**

BELOW Colchester Zoo, devoted to the preservation and conservation of a variety of endangered species and giving visitors easy-to-understand information through the latest technology.

ABOVE RIGHT Specialist lighting, exciting music and its superb maple floor make Rollerworld the finest rollerskating rink in Europe.

RIGHT Mediterranean-themed Aqua Springs; there is no other place quite like it in Britain to relax.

World. Here visitors can relax from the stresses and strains of modern life in a Mediterranean-themed sauna and spa.

Much of Colchester's long history can be found in the town's five museums. The flagship, **Colchester Castle Museum**, is inside the largest Norman keep ever built. A little-known fact is that the Tower of London was modelled on Colchester Castle. The museum's superb Roman collections are among the finest in the country.

Transformed in recent years, the museum now features interactive displays where visitors can try on a toga and touch real Roman pottery. Audio-visual presentations help

RIGHT **Savour the heady atmosphere of a traditional delicatessen at Gunton's.**

BELOW **Colchester Castle Museum – just the place to imagine life in Roman Colchester.**

understand how life works at a microscopic level in the Discovery Room. Natural History is also the theme at **High Woods Country Park**. This 134-hectare park was once part of a hunting-forest used by Henry VIII. Nowadays the country park contains woodland, grassland, farmland, a lake and a fully equipped visitor centre.

Nature lovers, and especially birdwatchers, should not miss the Essex Wildlife Trust's conservation centres at **Fingringhoe Wick** and **Abberton Reservoir**, which include nature trails, gift shops and displays.

Hollytrees, an elegant Georgian town-house situated on the edge of Castle Park, is now a museum where visitors can find out what their grandparents and their parents played with when they were children. The Mason Collection of Colchester-made clocks dating from the seventeenth to the nineteenth century can be found

visitors discover what life was like in the castle prisons and how it felt to live in Colchester during the eleven-week Civil War siege in 1648.

The **Natural History Museum** can be found just opposite the gates to Castle Park. Here visitors can guess what is inside the feely boxes and

RIGHT **Can visitors guess what is in the feely box at the Natural History Museum?**

in **Tymperleys**, a splendid fifteenth-century timber-framed house situated in the town centre.

A little further afield, at Chappel and Wakes Colne, is the **East Anglian Railway Museum**, which features the most comprehensive collection of period railway architecture and engineering in East Anglia.

Colchester is fortunate indeed to have an excellent range of shops. Quiet lanes of smaller, specialist shops and boutiques nestle alongside larger shopping centres where the 'big name' stores can be found. Colchester also has excellent leisure attractions in a temperate climate, with its location in East Anglia ensuring mild winters and warm, dry summers.

Colchester's economy in recent years has been noted for achieving a sensitive balance between vital growth and expansion while preserving the town's distinctive heritage and high quality of life.

The Borough has one of the fastest-growing economic bases and its location continues to attract new investment. Lying alongside the A12, the town is linked to the Midlands by

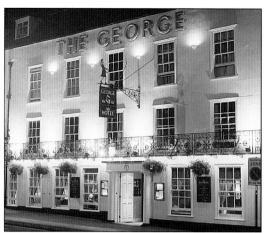

RIGHT One of Colchester's many quality hotels, which along with B&Bs and self-catering establishments, provide a much appreciated welcome for visitors from the UK and overseas.

BELOW Colchester boasts the region's premier business park, the 35-acre (14 ha) Colchester Business Park, home to many internationally known organisations.

the A14. Travelling east–west, the A120 Trans-European route passes through the Borough and the M11 and London Stansted International Airport less than one hour's drive to the west.

On the northern fringe of Colchester is the region's premier business centre, the Colchester Business Park, home to many internationally recognised companies.

The town's proximity to the east coast's two major Haven ports at Harwich and Felixstowe gives the town a commercial advantage which has been taken up by a number of leading companies. Colchester has preserved a flourishing manufacturing base that includes British Export Award-winning companies such as Woods Air Movement and Alstom Engines Ltd, Paxman, who consistently win multi-million pound contracts at home and abroad.

But Colchester has also embraced the new business technologies and is developing as a sub-regional call centre and as a renowned centre for the telecommunications, financial services, print and electronic industries.

The business and commercial scene in Colchester will see some exciting developments in the next few years, possibly including a new community

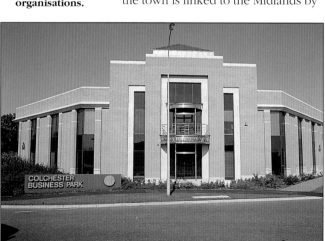

stadium to the north of the town. The development might include a stadium, hotel, conference and leisure and parking facilities, as well as a park and ride scheme.

A key area for the town's growth in the new millennium lies to the north of the town on the 280-acre (113 ha) site of the now-redundant Severalls Hospital. It is hoped that a new junction from the A12 to the north of the town would pave the way to the largest single development site in the Borough.

Colchester is a town of educational excellence, with the town's four major providers of post-sixteen education and training, the University of Essex, the Colchester Institute, the Adult Education Centre and the acclaimed Sixth Form College, increasingly working together to provide a comprehensive and easily accessible programme of lifelong learning in the town.
At secondary level, the town boasts two of the country's leading selective schools among many other outstanding institutions.

With a growing national emphasis on the need for a skilled and flexible workforce, Colchester benefits from the superb educational training, research and development programmes of its local educational centre, notably the 6000-student strong University of Essex which has been described as 'the most academically distinguished university in Britain for its size'.

LEFT The University of Essex, regarded as one of Britain's leading universities and recognised internationally for high standards of teaching and research. It is also Britain's most international university, hosting students from 109 countries.

LEFT AND ABOVE Culver Square and Lion Walk, just two of the many pedestrianised shopping areas in the town. With 'larger name' stores and smaller specialist shops in a compact town centre area, shopping in Colchester is a real treat.

Surrounding Area

Much of the beauty of the North Essex and East Anglian countryside lies in its variety: a unique combination of wide skies, gently rolling farmland, woodland, valleys, rivers and estuaries. The region's landscape has been an inspiration to artists for centuries. Indeed, perhaps the most enduring images of the Essex/Suffolk countryside were painted by John Constable in the early nineteenth century. The area where he grew up and painted throughout his life is now immortalised as **Constable Country**. East Bergholt, the artist's birthplace in 1776, is now a quiet village dominated by St Mary's Church, dating from the mid-fourteenth century, which unusually houses its bells in a cage in the churchyard. Nearby is **Flatford Mill**, owned by the National Trust, and the scene of Constable's most famous work, *The Hay Wain*.

The stunning altarpiece in St James' Church in the village of Nayland is another of Constable's legacies still in place today. Further into Suffolk, close to the picturesque wool town of Hadleigh is Kersey. With its streets lined by pastel-washed houses and a

ABOVE **Willy Lott's Cottage today. This pretty cottage by the River Stour was immortalised in *The Hay Wain*, perhaps Constable's most famous painting.**

ford complete with resident ducks, Kersey has been called 'the prettiest village in England'. Lavenham, nearby, is England's best-preserved medieval town and boasts the magnificent **Guildhall of Corpus Christi** dating from the early sixteenth century. The Guildhall features an exhibition of the local cloth industry through the centuries.

A stroll down the narrow lanes and streets reveals splendid timber-framed houses, pastel-painted cottages and craft, gift and tea shops. Back towards Colchester is Sudbury, a thriving market town where the weaving tradition dates back to the thirteenth century. Sudbury was the birthplace of the revered English landscape- and portrait-painter, Thomas Gainsborough, and **Gainsborough's House** features the largest collection of his work in any British gallery.

To the west of Colchester is the wool town of Braintree, home of the **Braintree Working Silk Museum** and the country's last remaining company of handloom silk-weavers. Today the sumptuous silk fabric is supplied to stately homes, royal households and for ceremonial robes.

BELOW **St Osyth's Abbey (also known as St Osyth's Priory) was founded in AD1121. Superbly constructed, it features perpendicular bands of squared flint, brick and stone. St Osyth's Abbey has been described in *Country Life* magazine as 'unexcelled in any monastic remains in the country'.**

Other buildings to note in Coggeshall are the twelfth-century **Coggeshall Abbey** and **Grange Barn** – the earliest in the country.

Colchester has had links with the sea throughout its history. The surrounding coast with its creeks and shallows provided ideal conditions for smuggling, whilst its link with oysters can be traced back to the Romans who cultivated oyster beds in the tidal estuaries nearby. Today our maritime heritage can be enjoyed at the picturesque riverside communities of Wivenhoe and Rowhedge, a visit which can be made from Colchester

Also nearby is **Cressing Temple**, where a pair of medieval timber-framed barns were built by the Knights Templar in the thirteenth century. Besides the wheat and barley barns are a Tudor granary and stables as well as an exhibition. The town of Coggeshall, once important in the trade of wool and lace and more recently made famous by television's *Lovejoy*, is now a major antiques centre with meandering streets and fine medieval half-timbered buildings such as **Paycocke's**, now owned by the National Trust.

ABOVE Copford's early twelfth-century church features a unique collection of recently restored frescoes showing a strong Byzantine influence in their content as well as technical excellence.

RIGHT The magnificent Guildhall of Corpus Christi in Lavenham dating from the early sixteenth century.

by cycle using the Wivenhoe Trail. A trip across the Strood (a long causeway that carries the road over a path originally constructed by the Saxons) leads to Mersea Island, a haven for water-sports enthusiasts and famous for its oyster fishery.

But the Essex coast is perhaps most famous for its seaside resorts. Clacton-on-Sea and Walton-on-the-Naze offer wide stretches of sandy beach, colourful gardens and parks, theatres and famous piers with all the traditional seaside attractions and entertainment. Nearby Frinton-on-Sea is well worth a visit for its timeless elegance.

Mistley, once home to Matthew Hopkins, the notorious Witchfinder

LEFT Small riverside communities are a feature of the nearby coast.

General in the seventeenth century, is now noted for its bevy of swans, towers designed by Robert Adam and pretty riverfront walks. To the east of nearby Manningtree there is the medieval seafaring town of Harwich which, with Dovercourt and Parkeston Quay, now provides modern visitors with a gateway to the Continent or their first glimpse of England.

ABOVE **Built around 1520, Layer Marney Tower is the country's tallest Tudor gatehouse. The 24-metre (80 ft) tower is well worth the climb for the spectacular views of the surrounding Essex countryside.**

North of Harwich is 40 miles (64 km) of Suffolk coastline that has been designated as 'Heritage Coast', being largely unspoilt and remote. Aldeburgh and Southwold are two small, secluded seaside towns of peaceful and period charm. Maritime heritage in Essex can also be discovered in the major yachting centres of Burnham-on-Crouch, Brightlingsea, Mersea and Maldon, where the famous Thames sailing-barges are moored.

ABOVE **Nearby Tiptree is home to the world-famous Wilkin's 'Tiptree' jams, preserves and conserves. Wilkin's also offer visitors a delightful museum featuring the history of jam-making in the village as well as a superb tearoom.**

BELOW **Sunset over Mersea Island, a haven for water-sports enthusiasts.**